T0358480

# Economics and Human Behaviour

First published in 1927, *Economics and Human Behaviour* is a defence of orthodox economics against the attacks of social psychology. The author has explicated on the characteristics and value of both orthodox economics as well as psychology, and then presented psychology's criticism against orthodox economics. Before concluding with the limitations of both disciplines, this tiny book reinstates the importance of orthodox economics in the gathering and interpretation of facts. Given the predominance of economics over psychology in current times, this book will be an interesting read for anyone keen on imagining the tables turned. It will also appeal to students of economics, history and psychology.

# Economics and Human Behaviour
## A Rejoinder to Social Psychologists

P. Sargant Florence

Routledge
Taylor & Francis Group

First published in 1927
by Kegan Paul, Trench, Trubner & Co. Ltd

This edition first published in 2022 by Routledge
4 Park Square, Milton Park, Abingdon, Oxon, OX14 4RN
and by Routledge
605 Third Avenue, New York, NY 10017

*Routledge is an imprint of the Taylor & Francis Group, an informa business*

© Kegan Paul, 1927

**Publisher's Note**
The publisher has gone to great lengths to ensure the quality of this reprint but points out that some imperfections in the original copies may be apparent.

**Disclaimer**
The publisher has made every effort to trace copyright holders and welcomes correspondence from those they have been unable to contact.

A Library of Congress record exists under LCCN: 28026347

ISBN: 978-1-032-30609-4 (hbk)
ISBN: 978-1-003-30652-8 (ebk)
ISBN: 978-1-032-30763-3 (pbk)

Book DOI 10.4324/9781003306528

# ECONOMICS

### AND

# HUMAN BEHAVIOUR

## A REJOINDER TO SOCIAL
## PSYCHOLOGISTS

BY

### P. SARGANT FLORENCE

*Lecturer in Economics, Magdalene College, Cambridge*
*Author of " The Economics of Fatigue and Unrest "*
*" Over-Population ", etc.*

LONDON:

KEGAN PAUL, TRENCH, TRUBNER & Co. Ltd.
BROADWAY HOUSE, CARTER LANE, E.C.
1927

*Printed in Great Britain by*
R. I. SEVERS, CAMBRIDGE

# CONTENTS

# CONTENTS

# PREFACE

At a time when business crises, industrial depressions, financial deadlocks, labour troubles, and trade wars follow thick and fast, it may seem pusillanimous for an economist to engage in discussion on the relations between rival theories of human behaviour. I venture to think, however, that these practical difficulties will not be permanently overcome without the co-operation of all the sciences that claim to study man. The very theory which purports to be the most exact and the most nearly related to these present difficulties is cried upon and isolated; doubts multiply over the whole conception of human mentality adopted by orthodox economics; and all the superstructure of laws and principles deduced therefrom are called contrary to human experience.

# ECONOMICS AND BEHAVIOUR

In his *Introduction to Social Psychology*, McDougall calls it "a libel not altogether devoid of truth to say that the classical political economy was a tissue of false conclusions drawn from false psychological assumptions"; and modern historians, anthropologists, sociologists, and publicists generally, all appear to join the psychologist in suspecting economic reasoning and the premises upon which that reasoning is based.

This suspicion is partly the result of the economist's apparent insensibility to criticism and his unabated devotion to the abstractions and mysteries of the cult practised in such sanctuaries as Cambridge ; and partly it is the result of highly seasoned tidbits of economic theory served up by psychologists and other non-economists for their own delectation. This essay starts, therefore, (Chapter I) by presenting an ungarnished carcass of economics that a psychologist can really get his teeth into. Other economists may not agree that this is the true structure and

## PREFACE

inwardness of economic thought (though I quote as far as possible from recognized authorities), or they may omit the whole section as stale news; but at least they, and my readers generally, are given the chance of knowing what I mean by economic orthodoxy and the economic standpoint.

The precise line of criticism to which this substance of economics is subject will be traced (Chapter II) as far as possible in the words of social psychologists themselves. The attack has often been adumbrated in handbooks of social psychology, but its implications have not been sufficiently surveyed by English economists, and attempts to defend the position do not (Chapter III) appear adequate. This essay is largely an attempt to assess the degree of damage inflicted and the amount of salvage that can be definitely retrieved.

Orthodox economic theory may prove a useful hypothesis to interpret the facts—but only after the facts are gathered, are related to the prevailing habits and institutions of the time and place, and are, wherever possible, statistically summarized.

The facts so arranged probably can be seldom interpreted on strictly hedonist premises ; and to serve any scientific purpose economic theories must be worded independently of utilitarian views (Chapter IV) to shed all implications that " men always act from self-interest ". Macaulay explained this—his own phrase— to mean " only that men, if they can, will do as they choose ", and certainly unless economics bases its terms upon less dogmatic conceptions of human springs to action (Chapter V), its laws will prove useless even as interpretative hypotheses.

Reconstructed upon broader lines, economics may turn upon the theory of social psychology, and demand its precise intentions (Chapter VI) in the interpretation of the habits and facts of human behaviour. Hereupon the exponent of instincts is revealed as a likely successor to the utilitarian

## PREFACE

as the villain of the piece, with methods
equally mysterious and deductive. The
plot thickens. Eventually (Chapter
VII) a happy conclusion comes in
sight, in which the limits of mere
psychological theory and of mere
observation of facts are recognized,
while both are found to play a necessary
part in searching the causes of our
social discontents.

# I

## ECONOMIC ORTHODOXY

It might be supposed that the science of Economics—née Political Economy—had lived long and respectably enough for economists to have agreed what exactly was their chief interest. Yet in their own opening chapters, economists define their subject in the most varied terms; and most of them unfortunate. The 'study of wealth' is inconclusive until we are told to what wealth refers, and the subsequent definition of wealth often leads us round in a circle, by reference to 'economic goods'. The 'science of human or social welfare or well-being' hardly avoids ethical and unscientific implications. The 'study of human needs' fails to distinguish economics from psychology, dietetics, architecture, or the sartorial art.

12

## ECONOMIC ORTHODOXY

A more certain indication of the scope of economics than such formal introductory definitions of text books[1] is to be found in their tables of contents.

With the exception of the chapters on taxation (the *compulsory* transference of wealth), all the divisions that figure in the contents can be considered as parts of one general problem, namely, why, under conditions of *voluntary* exchange on a market, goods, services, and factors of production exchange at the value, prices, rates of wages, interest, profits, etc. at which they do exchange. The main subject of economics is, in short, the terms of exchange.[2]

Orthodox economics professes to

[1] A further definition is discussed below, III, page 52.

[2] For the sake of bringing the conception home to the reader I shall use the phrase '*prices and* terms of exchange' or simply ' prices ' without taking sides, however, (Cf. Cassell's *Fundamental Thoughts in Economics*) on the question whether or not exchange-values are the heart of the matter apart from the money-prices in which those values are usually exhibited.

13

study this subject scientifically in the indicative, not the imperative or optative mood of ethics; and in this spirit, pure of moral implications, it has set up an apparatus of thought for regular use in answering its problems. The salient fact seized upon is that, although in any one market the price at any one time of one quality of article is usually the same to all comers, the several units bought or sold at this same price may not have been produced under equally favourable conditions, nor are they likely to be consumed with exactly the same relish. More accurately, the supply-price (at which people are able and willing to produce) and the demand-price (at which people want and can afford to purchase) are likely to be different for different units of the same services or goods, though each unit of the same sort must actually sell in one market for the same price.

But though the price paid and received for most units is not necessarily the same as their demand-price and

14

supply-price, this actual price is influenced by demand and supply; would-be buyers will not pay more than their demand-price and would-be sellers will not take less than their supply-price.

To reach the conditions underlying actual prices, i.e. the money passing hands, the conditions determining demand-price and supply-price must be separately investigated. Demand and supply are to the economist merely 'sides' along either of which the concrete conditions likely to affect price can be ranged. The formulation of an answer to an economic problem in terms of supply and demand is simply the opening of the game, much as a 'gambit' is to the chess-player. Novelty of treatment is sacrificed to secure a systematic inquiry into all the possibly relevant conditions, just as in courts of law it is, I believe, a rule of procedure to hear separately and as a whole the plaintiff's case and then the defendant's, and only gradually, by a sort of pendulum swing between the two, to narrow down the issue.

And the economists also eventually narrow down the issue. To make any consistent interpretation of prices and the terms of exchange, the forces of supply and demand are brought into some sort of relation with one another. They are fused to form one general principle from which all economic phenomena may be deduced.

For this purpose economics makes the presumption that a sufficiently large proportion of human beings base their demand-prices and supply-prices for various amounts of goods and services upon the ' *utility* ' of these commodities in consumption and the ' *cost* ' of these commodities in production ; and that this sufficient proportion of persons make a sufficient proportion of their purchases or sales by calculating cost and utility and balancing one against the other.[1] Calculation on

[1] It is not necessary for orthodox economics to assume that everybody always calculates what amounts to buy or sell when the price

the part of these ' economic men ' does not imply that the exact degree of cost or degree of utility can be given in so many numbers of ' units ', but that there is a rough appreciation of what is worth while and not worth while, and of what combination of different products can (through the principle of substituting units of one for units of another) yield greatest utility for given costs.

ruling in the market is at various given levels. Henderson puts the position clearly. (Cf. *Supply and Demand*, pp. 45-6) "Those of us who do not bother about the price we pay for our ties and collars owe a debt of gratitude, of which we are insufficiently conscious, to the more careful people who do ; as well as to the custom which prevails in shops in Western countries (as distinct from the bazaars of the East) of charging as a rule a uniform price to all customers. If *we* were the only people who bought these things, an enterprising salesman would be able to charge us very much what he chose. He could put up his price, and we would hardly be aware of it. And, as by lowering his price he could not tempt us to buy more, price reductions would be few and far between. But fortunately there are always some people who do know what the price is, even when they are buying collars and ties ; and who will adjust the amount they buy in accordance with the price. It is these worthy people who make the laws of demand work out as we well know they do. It is

17

## ECONOMICS AND BEHAVIOUR

In ' production for use and not for
profit ', ' Robinson Crusoe economy ',
or amateur blackberrying it is the
same person who is incurring the cost
of being pricked, smudged, overloaded,
and who is presumably getting utility
therefrom. But in the current economics of the market-place the producers
and the consumers of any one article

they who will curtail their consumption if
the price has risen and it is they who con-
stitute the seller's problem, and help to keep
down prices for the rest of us. The rest of
us—it is well to be quite blunt about it—
simply do not count in this connection."

But Henderson is careless in writing a few
lines further on as though the one purchaser
exactly at the margin were sufficient to
determine price. " Just as it is the marginal
purchase, so it is the marginal purchaser who
matters. It is the man who, before he buys a
motor bicycle, weighs the matter up very carefully indeed and only just decides to buy it,
whose demand affects the price of motor
bicycles." At every price there will probably
be some buyer on the margin, and it is rather
the grouping of demand prices near (above or
below) the margin, the ' elasticity ' of demand
of the ' near-marginal ' men, that exerts a
determining influence on price. A price
might well be lowered to meet a large group
of demands just below the old price ; con-
trariwise it might be raised if only a few sales
would be lost thereby.

18

or service are different persons or organizations ; and the calculation of the amount to be bought or sold is not a balancing of utility against cost in the mind of one person, but is a balancing in the minds of prospective *buyers* or *consumers* of approximate *utility* of various amounts against the price ruling on the market, and is a balancing in the minds of prospective *sellers* or *producers* of approximate *costs* of various amounts against the price ruling on the market.

Now the economist considers that the utility per unit of the commodity diminishes for the consumer (by the law of diminishing utility) with the increased amount of units purchased, and that at every price there must be theoretically some amount of units where the additional utility obtained by adding one unit is calculated by buyers (or at least roughly appreciated) as about balancing the price per unit ruling on the market. At this amount the calculating consumer is hailed as on the ' margin of doubt ' whether or not to

19

buy an additional unit, and this possibly additional unit that may 'tip the balance' is acclaimed as having a *marginal utility*.

Similarly from the producers' point of view, a given productive capacity, personal or material, may be unable at any one time to produce more than a certain amount of services or articles without increasing costs right up to the price ruling on the market ; and here also there will be, for every price ruling, a margin of doubt, a marginal unit, and a marginal cost of production.

Though on the market the balancing of utility and cost occurs indirectly through a mutual reference by different individuals to the price ruling, the balancing process still holds good. The receipt or possible receipt of the price by the producer in exchange for his costs represents to him a source of *utility*, and the payment of the price by the consumer in exchange for utility represents to him a *cost* in the shape of the loss of means probably gained at some trouble to himself.

## ECONOMIC ORTHODOXY

There are many sciences concerned with methods of production and supply —agricultural botany, physics, and chemistry ; and many others— dietetics, hygiene, aesthetics—dealing with consumption and the content of demand. But the standpoint of economic science is sharply differentiated from these in *weighing* the probable cost of production against its probable utility in consumption. It is not sufficient to assert that such or such foods are wholesome to consume and can be produced in such and such ways ; if society is to be economically activated the persons who are to produce and the persons who are to consume must appreciate, consciously or unconsciously, that there is a positive balance of utility, or at least no adverse balance, in striking the mutual bargain.

Whenever an economist uses the auxiliary verb ' can ' he is thinking not of technical or physical possibilities, but of the probability of a balance of utility over cost (or at least the

absence of any adverse balance)
accruing to either party in the transaction.

Vines *can* be grown in Scotland,
says the horticulturist, if green houses
are erected and properly heated. No
doubt, answers the economist, but
the cost of heating and maintaining
greenhouses, let alone the expense
of their erection, far out-balances the
returns obtainable on the wine market,
and therefore as an economic proposition vines *cannot* be grown. The
conditions of their supply and the
conditions of their demand are such
that the sales cannot meet expenses.
And here there can be no probable
possible *margin* of doubt, no possible
doubt whatever.

This may appear trite enough, yet
some of the leading opponents of the
trite seem sadly to have missed the
point. In his *Proposed Roads to Free-
dom* Mr. Bertrand Russell, quoting
Kropotkin, tells us that by methods
of intensive cultivation already in
actual operation, the amount of food

produced on a given area can be increased far beyond anything that most uninformed persons suppose possible. The usual instances are cited of enormous and repeated crops per acre, but not a single mention is made of the costs of manure, greenhouses, and additional labour involved by intensive cultivation[1]—costs that may entirely outbalance the added revenue obtainable in selling the *additional* produce raised by their means.

The margin of doubt most worrisome to the hesitating purchaser or seller often occurs, not in balancing a simple utility against a simple cost, but as a ' margin of indifference ' between two balances.

Suppose I am asked to deliver at a given stipend a series of extension lectures some distance away during

[1] These items of expense are heavy, and are ever present in the practical cultivator's mind. Cf. Nelson's *Encyclopaedia of Agriculture*, article on " Intensive Cultivation ".

the course of the University term, and suppose my resources in time and energy are limited. How as an economic man, am I supposed to set about forming a decision? I should first set the cost of the venture against the utility of the stipend. This cost will include the actual effort of preparing and delivering the lectures and the fatigue of the journey, and also the sacrifice of the opportunities for obtaining utility from fees earned in intra-mural University teaching for which I would have no time or energy to spare if I indulged in extra-mural work.

But University teaching also has costs to set against its fees. I am therefore confronted by a quadrilateral or four-termed comparison, a balancing of a balance of costs and utilities against another balance of costs and utilities; and this is the form in which the economic man usually has to think out his problems where resources and working time and energy are fixed and limited.

## ECONOMIC ORTHODOXY

Every act involves some utility and some cost, and a *choice* often has to be made between acts, all of which entail a balance of utility. In that case the course that is chosen may be said to involve a sacrifice of the balance of utility entailed in the alternative course of action which has the next greatest balance of utility, and this may be and has been referred to in English textbooks as the *real* cost of the course chosen.[1] But it is a confusing use of words, and the use of the earlier American phrase, alternative cost[2] or opportunity cost,[3] would leave real cost to refer solely to more primary physiological or psychological aversions. Indeed Marshall's phrase " efforts and sacrifices " seems adequately to cover the case. To be balanced against utilities there are not merely psychophysiological efforts and a sacrifice of

[1] E.g. Henderson, *Supply and Demand,* Chap. X.

[2] Fetter, *Principles of Economics,* 3rd edition, pp. 274, 277.

[3] Davenport, *Economics of Enterprise,* Chap. VI.

present pleasure by postponing satisfactions and ' saving ', but also a
sacrifice of all alternate opportunities ;
and the margin of doubt may well occur
in balancing one utility merely against
the sacrifice of another.

Hitherto the economist has allowed
himself to assume that a price
ruling on the market is given, and has
concentrated on the reactions to such
a price occurring in the amounts
supplied and demanded by producers
(sellers) and consumers (buyers). But
price itself may react to the supply
and demand situation, and it is with
the study of price-reactions that we
enter the inner precincts of economic
science.

Reactions in the price actually paid
for any exchangeable article (goods,
services, and factors of production)
are assumed to occur in a market as
a result of changes in the aggregate
amount of the article demanded by competing buyers at the various demand-
prices, and/or as a result of changes

in the aggregate amount of the article supplied by competing sellers at the various supply-prices. These demand-prices and supply-prices for various amounts of the article remain the result of a sufficient number of persons balancing utility and costs respectively against price paid or received.

And it is only after such independently determined schedules of demand-prices and supply-prices are imagined that those definitely economic laws of supply and demand, which Henderson[1] prints in leaded type, can be affirmed.

> I. 'When, at the price ruling, demand exceeds supply, the price tends to rise. Conversely, when supply exceeds demand, the price tends to fall."

> II. " A rise in price tends, sooner or later, to decrease demand and to increase supply. Conversely a fall in price tends, sooner or later, to increase demand and to decrease supply."

> III. " Price tends to the level at which demand is equal to supply."

This third law follows from the other two.

[1] Henderson, *Supply and Demand*, Chap. II.

" Supposing that demand is in excess of supply, then the price will tend to rise. After the price has risen, the supply will become larger, while the demand will fall away. The excess of demand with which we started will thus clearly be diminished. But if there remains any portion of this excess, the same reactions will continue ; the price will rise further, and for the same reason ; demand will be further checked and supply further stimulated. In other words, these forces must persist until the entire excess of demand over supply is eliminated. If we start by supposing supply to exceed demand, the converse chain of sequences will operate."

These three laws are, according to Henderson, the corner-stone of economic theory. And he declares that these laws can be arrived at independently without reference to psychological assumptions ; in fact it is not till his sixth law is enunciated[1] that the prevailing trend towards an equilibrium of demand and supply exhibited by the ' corner-stone ' laws is traced back to considerations of cost and utility.

[1] " A commodity tends to be produced on a scale at which its marginal cost of production is equal to its marginal utility, as measured in terms of money, and both are equal to its price." Op. cit. Chap. IV.

# ECONOMIC ORTHODOXY

This declaration of independence will be dealt with later (Chapter IV). It is hardly orthodox ; and the case of economic orthodoxy is more fitly closed and summarized by Dr. Marshall's ' outline ' statement of this economic corner-stone in which he avoids reference to price ruling on the market but clearly exhibits the calculation of ' worth-whileness ' continually implied.[1]

When " the amount produced (in a unit of time) is such that the demand price is greater than the supply price, then sellers receive more than is sufficient to make it worth their while to bring goods to market to that amount ; and there is at work an active force tending to increase the amount brought forward for sale. On the other hand, when the amount produced is such that the demand price is less than the supply price, sellers receive less than is sufficient to make it worth their while to bring goods to market on that scale ; so that those who

[1] Marshall, *Principles of Economics*, V, iii, 6.

were just on the margin of doubt as
to whether to go on producing are
decided not to do so, and there is an
active force at work tending to diminish
the amount brought forward for sale.
When the demand price is equal to
the supply price, the amount produced
has no tendency either to be increased
or to be diminished ; it is in equilibrium."

## II

## THE PSYCHOLOGISTS' ATTACK

Orthodox Economics, then, is an attempt to interpret events in human behaviour (prices and terms of exchange) by reference to *calculated balancing of utilities against costs* by considerable numbers of producers and consumers. The word ' interpret ' conveys the impression that the events are known and only require explaining. This is not the actual procedure of economics. On the contrary, it is man's processes of calculation and balancing that are taken as known, and past events are reconstructed or future events predicted from the circumstances of the time, in accordance with these ' known ' processes. In case the results of such *deduction* should conflict with patent facts of the actual world the title of ' normal ' is bestowed upon

31

them. Such conflicts are, however, deprecated ; and it is recognized that the general conception of human calculation from which deduction is made is subject to modification in the interests of truth, so as to maintain some rough correspondence between the normal and the humdrum but real.

And recently the reality of the old conception of human mentality has been insistently questioned. The large majority of human beings are believed not to calculate deliberately in most of their actions what is the balance of utility and cost to them ; they act, according to one school, on their ideas of right and wrong, according to another, on their instincts.

In Dr. Marshall's heyday the champions of the power of conscience were the more formidable, at any rate in Cambridge.[1] Dr. Marshall was at

[1] " As recently as the year 1893 the late Professor H. Sidgwick . . . assumed that moral or reasonable action is normal and natural to man in virtue of some vaguely conceived principle, and in all seriousness wrote an

pains to show that " everyone who is worth anything carries his higher nature with him into business "[1] ; and in a presidential address to Section F of the British Association he said he looked forward to an economic chivalry on the part of employers in solving industrial problems. It was fashionable also to meet the charge of dogmatism by citing Professor Wagner's list of human motives, at least in a footnote or appendix.[2] The motive least intermittent in its action was still held to be " the striving for one's own economic advantage, and the fear of one's economic need ". This motive was generally taken to form the cash-nexus between the supplier (the producer or worker) and the demander

article to prove that ' unreasonable action ' is possible and is actually achieved occasionally, and to explain if possible this strange anomalous fact." McDougall, *Introduction to Social Psychology*, p. 8.

[1] Marshall, *Principles of Economics*, I, ii, 1.

[2] Keynes, *Scope and Method of Political Economy*, footnote p. 128 ; Marshall, *Principles of Economics*, Appendix D.

(the customer or employer); but three other egoistic motives and one that was 'altruistic' in nature were also taken into account, as forming a nexus 'pulling' work out of people and attaching supply to a demand. There is the love of work, the hobby or sport nexus; there is the feeling of honour and the striving for recognition and approval, the fame-or-shame nexus connected with a system of prizes rather than prices; and there is the fear of punishment and hope of reward, the beat-or-treat nexus. The altruistic motive may be called the duty nexus; and it was described as " the impelling force of the inward command to moral action, the pressure of the feeling of duty, and the fear of one's own inward blame, that is, of the gnawings of conscience ".

Marshall's *Principles of Economics* contains no reference to instinct in the index; but certainly it is the champions of the power of human instinct, rather than those of deliberate motives, conscience, or inward com-

34

mand, who are to-day in the ascendant ;
and it is important to examine the
grounds of their contention.

The tendency exhibited by Bentham
to treat all behaviour as the result of
deliberate calculation is generally referred to by modern psychologists
as the ' rationalist ' or the ' intel-
lectualist ' fallacy.[1] And the minds
of the moral philosophers such as
Bentham, Mill, and Sidgwick, upon
whose " curious views " " the social
sciences were largely founded " are
considered by McDougall to have
been either " constitutionally devoid
of the powerful impulses that so often
move ordinary men to actions which
they know to be morally wrong and
against their true interests and destruc-
tive of their happiness, or so completely
moralized by strict self-discipline that
these powerful impulses are completely
subordinated and hardly make themselves felt ".

[1] R. H. Thouless, *Social Psychology* , p.181 ;
S.  S.  Brierley, *Introduction  to  Psychology*,
Chap.  IV.

## ECONOMICS AND BEHAVIOUR

To those who are initiated into social psychology, economic text-books must seem as naïve in their references to human prudence, resolution, desire for happiness, and conscious calculation to obtain the same, as the similar treatment of the life and problems of redbreasts for the edification of Early Victorian children seems to the ordinary Georgian adult of to-day.[1]

> " The hen redbreast laid four eggs, and then took her seat upon them, resolving that nothing should tempt her to leave the nest for any length of time till she had hatched her infant brood. At length the day arrived when the happy mother heard the chirping of her little ones ; with inexpressible tenderness she pressed them to her bosom and presented them to her mate, who viewed them with rapture, and seated himself by her side that he might share her pleasure.
>
> " ' We may promise ourselves much delight in rearing our little family ', said he, ' but it will give us a great deal of trouble. I would willingly bear the whole myself, but it will be impossible for me, with my utmost labour and industry, to supply all our nestlings with what is sufficient for their daily support ; it will therefore be necessary for you to leave the nest sometimes to seek provisions for them.'

[1] *The Robin Redbreasts* ; *Designed to Teach Children the Proper Treatment of Animals*, by Mrs. Trimmer, Chap. 1.

# THE PSYCHOLOGISTS' ATTACK

> " She declared . . . she had dis-
> covered a place . . . where food was
> scattered on purpose for such birds as
> would take the pains of seeking it.
> " ' This is a lucky discovery indeed for
> us ', replied her mate, ' for this great
> increase of family renders it prudent to
> make use of every means for supplying
> our necessities.' "

But are not human beings, urges the psychologist, almost as far from acting on such rationally argued prudential grounds as the robin-redbreasts ? Will not man's instincts underlie his behaviour almost as effectively as they are now generally admitted to determine the behaviour of other animals ?

By the journalist, the politician, the theologian, and the moral scientist, McDougall points out, the words instinct and instinctive are commonly used—like references to a woman's intuition—decently to cloak a writer's attempts to explain any individual or collective action that he fails, or has not tried, to understand.[1] But

---

[1] William James also resents this vague use of the word. " The older writings on instinct are ineffectual waste of words,

among professed psychologists, continues McDougall, " there is now fair agreement as to the usage of the terms instinct and instinctive ", and he defines instinct as " an inherited or innate physical disposition which determines its possessor to perceive, and to pay attention to, objects of a certain class, to experience an emotional excitement of a particular quality upon perceiving such an object, and to act in regard to it in a particular manner, or at least to experience an impulse to such action ".[1]

Other psychologists do not agree about the emotional " excitement of a particular quality " ; and the use of instinct to refer to an act or an

because their authors smothered everything in vague wonder at the clairvoyant and prophetic power of the animals so superior to anything in man—and at the beneficence of God in endowing them with such a gift. But God's beneficence endows them, first of all with a nervous system ; and turning our attention to this makes instinct appear neither more nor less wonderful than all the other facts of life."

[1] McDougall, *Introduction to Social Psychology*, Chap. II.

impulse to act, is the more important feature of the definition for the layman to mark. An instinct is a ' reaction ', but differs from mere reflex action by " its greater complexity of organization. While a reflex action is a response of a group of muscles to a stimulus, an instinctive reaction is a response (which may involve the whole of the organism) to a situation."[1]

The particular manner of the reaction is so marked, the sequence of action recurs so persistently, that the word ' pattern ' is often applied ; and Watson defines instinct as an hereditary pattern reaction or " a combination of explicit congenital responses unfolding serially under appropriate stimulation ". A baby about a hundred days old will, for instance, invariably " respond to a rapid threatening movement of the hand or some other object as follows : a definite sharp blink of the eyes, an upward movement of the hands, and

[1] R. H. Thouless, *Social Psychology*, Chap. II.

a backward movement of the head "[1]
—apparently a trefoil pattern.

The instinctive behaviour of an animal is most certainly not ' undertaken ' for some *calculated* (positive or negative) balance of utility over cost. The cat does not pursue mice or run away from a dog with the thought of a meal or of death in mind. " He is just born with a nervous system so constructed that when the moving object we call a mouse appears in his field of vision, he must pursue it, and when the object giving a different series of stimuli, which we call a dog, appears, he must run away."[2] And robins don't sit on eggs because they like having children and know or find by experience that this is the most successful plan. It is either a manifestation of the parental instinct, or, as a recent French psychologist claims,[3] it is due to a local irritation which can

[1] J. B. Watson, *Psychology*, Chap. VII.

[2] Z. C. Dickinson, *Economic Motives*, p. 99.

[3] Cf. C. K. Ogden, *The Meaning of Psychology*, Chap. VII.

40

be assuaged only by sitting on the cool surface of an egg.

The major human instincts according to McDougall are those of flight, repulsion, curiosity, and pugnacity, which are accompanied by the emotions of fear, disgust, wonder, and anger, respectively, and the parental and the self-assertive and self-abasement instincts. These latter two are perhaps the political instincts *par excellence*.

The tendency to accumulate wealth, and most specifically economic behaviour, is taken by psychologists as the outcome in the main of the acquisitive instinct.[1] And though McDougall considers this instinct, displayed so eminently by jackdaws and squirrels, as only one among many, and in social behaviour generally rather a minor instinct at that, Ellwood endorses the socialists'[2] contention that the present social organization im-

[1] McDougall, *Introduction to Social Psychology*, p. 324 ; Thouless, *op. cit.* p. 286.

[2] C. A. Ellwood, *Sociology in its Psychological Aspects*.

mensely stimulates this instinct of acquisition and causes all sorts of needless exaggerations. Civilized man in his opinion is " having this instinct bred into him perhaps more than any other quality by the process of selection now going on in society."

Carleton Parker was perhaps the pioneer in the application of the psychology of instincts to economic activities, and his study of the California casual labourer is a *locus classicus* in economic methodology.

> " If we postulate some sixteen instinct unit characters which are present under the laborer's blouse and insistently demand the same gratification that is, with painful care, planned for the college student, in just what kind of perverted compensations must a laborer indulge to make endurable his existence ? A western hobo tries in a more or less frenzied way to compensate for a general all-embracing thwarting of his nature by a wonderful concentration of sublimation activities on the wander instinct. The monotony, indignity, dirt, and sexual apologies of, for instance, the unskilled worker's life bring their definite fixations, their definite irrational, inferiority obsessions.
>
> " The balked laborer here follows one of the two described lines of conduct :

First, he either weakens, becomes inefficient, drifts away, loses interest in the quality of his work, drinks, deserts his family ; or secondly, he indulges in a true type inferiority compensation, and in order to dignify himself, to eliminate for himself his inferiority in his own eyes, he strikes or brings on a strike ; he commits violence, or he stays on the job and injures machinery or mutilates the materials. He is a fit food for dynamite conspiracies. He is ready to make sabotage a part of his regular habit scheme. His condition is one of mental stress and unfocused psychic unrest, and could in all accuracy be called a definite industrial psychosis. He is neither wilful nor responsible, he is suffering from a stereotyped mental disease."[1]

Carleton Parker devotes a paragraph to the economic significance of each of the sixteen ' unit ' instincts which he ' postulates '. Two sample paragraphs are worth quoting.

" *Instinct of leadership and mastery*. It often appears that man seeks leadership and mastery solely because their acquisition places him in a better position to gratify his other instinctive promptings. But there also seems a special gratification in leading and mastery for their own sake. Modern life shows prodigious effort, paid only in the state of being a boss of the gang, a 'leading' college

[1] Carleton Parker, *The Casual Laborer and Other Essays*, pp. 162-3.

man, a ' prominent ' citizen, a secretary or a vice-president, a militia captain or a church elder. A secret ambition to some day lead some group on some quest, be it ethical or economic, is planted deep in our nature. Every dog longs to have his day."

" *Instinct of display* : *vanity* : *ostentation*. This old disposition gives the basic concept for Veblen's remarkable analysis of the economic activities of America's leisure class. The particular state of the industrial arts with its trust control and divorce of producer and consumer, plus political peace, has taken from man his ancient opportunity to show his unique gifts in ownership of economic goods and in valor. So he is driven in his yearning for attention to perverted activities. He lives to waste conspicuously, wantonly, originally, and, by the refined uselessness of his wasting, to show to the gaping world what an extraordinary person he is. The sensitiveness of social matrons to mention in the society columns, the hysteria to be identified with the changing vagaries of the style, the fear of identification with drab and useful livelihoods, offer in their infinite variety a multitude of important economic phenomena."[1]

Contemporaneously Professor Irving Fisher published a list of seven fundamental human instincts, with hints as to how employers could help " the worker satisfy " them—all on a single

[1] Op. cit. p. 151-153.

sheet of foolscap convenient for pasting on the employer's wall ; and Ordway Tead devoted an entire book to *Instincts in Industry*, and sought manifestations of fifteen of them in as many chapters.

That men will stand in line in the American equivalent of teashops waiting for ' my waitress ' is taken as an instance of the sex-instinct, though, as a reviewer remarked, more will stand in line waiting for ' my barber '.[1] More ingenious is the assignment of the case of workmen going on strike against their convictions of justice, to the paternal instinct ; and the case of workmen reluctant to transfer from one forge to another, to the instinct of possession.

Such instances may seem somewhat trivial. Yet the most orthodox of economists have admitted the important rôle that ' mere ' psychology plays in financial crises and business panics, and the herd-instinct observable among

[1] Review by Leon Ardzrooni in the *Political Science Quarterly*, March, 1920.

cattle and sheep seems to explain these economic facts.

Mechanical invention plays a most important rôle in modern economics ; but inventors are notoriously prone to invent with little calculation as to their probable financial success, and to go on fiddling with their machines by a sort of instinct of manipulation or workmanship.

Again, many successful advertisements are not designed to form conscious desires in prospective purchasers —desires upon which the ' prospect ' as a normal economic man is supposed to build his demand schedule, but are designed to break down his calculated ' resistance ' to making a purchase. Such advertisements, including the display of the proffered commodity itself, aim their shafts at man's and woman's impulsive reactions to bright, coloured, fluffy, lacy, furry objects ; to emotional verbal appeals ; to style and fashion ; to good fellowship in the sight of bottled intoxicants ; reactions to the tune of, I *must* have

46

it ! Have another ! *She's* got one !
Won't they be green with envy !
They're wearing them ! Everybody's
doing it !

Labels and trade names are as
important as the quality and price of
the goods or services labelled and
named.

> " The modern manufacturer, jobber,
> and dealer find that complicated psycho-
> logical and social demands require that
> crackers, eggs, tea, clothespins, chewing-
> gum, automobiles, pianos, furniture,
> insurance companies, and international
> enterprises must each and all be christ-
> ened, marked with a recognizable symbol,
> encased in a distinctive package, or
> indicated by special devices in the form
> of brand, color, marking, emblem, or
> stationery."[1]

Graham Wallas elaborates an imagin-
ary case.

> " The actual tea leaves in the world
> are as varied and unstable as the actual
> political opinions of mankind. Every
> leaf in every tea-garden is different
> from every other leaf, and a week of
> damp weather may change the whole
> stock in any warehouse. What there-
> fore should the advertiser do to create
> a commercial ' entity ', a ' tea ' which

[1] H. L. Hollingworth and A. T. Poffen-
berger, *Applied Psychology*, p. 235.

men can think and feel about? . . .
Nowadays . . . . such an advertiser would
practice on our automatic and subconscious associations. He would choose
some term, say 'Paramatta Tea',
which would produce in most men a
vague suggestion of the tropical East,
combined with the subconscious memory
of a geography lesson on Australia. He
would then proceed to create in connection with the word an automatic
picture-image having previous emotional
associations of its own. By the time
that a hundred thousand pounds had
been cleverly spent, no one in England
would be able to see the word 'Paramatta' on a parcel without a vague impulse to buy, founded on a day-dream
recollection of his grandmother, or of the
British fleet, or of a pretty young
English matron, or of any other subject
that the advertiser had chosen for its
association with the emotions of trust
and affection."[1]

## Instances need not be multiplied.

" If a man " suggests Graham Wallas,
" were followed through one ordinary
day, without his knowing it, by a
cinematographic camera and a phono-
graph, and if all his acts and sayings
were reproduced before him next day,
he would be astonished to find how few
of them were the result of a deliberate
search for the means of attaining ends.
He would, of course, see that much of
his activity consisted in the half-

[1] Graham Wallas, *Human Nature in
Politics*, Chap. II.

conscious repetition, under the influence
of habit, of movements which were
originally more fully conscious. But
even if all cases of habit were excluded
he would find that only a small proportion
of the residue could be explained as
being directly produced by an intellectual
calculation."[1]

Enough has been quoted to indicate
the forces that have rallied to Dr.
McDougall's banner. A new psychological school of economists and political
scientists has been proclaimed among
his disciples, and has, in the course
of its progress, gathered to itself
psychological and economic theories
of similar shades. Carleton Parker
exhibits the marks of readings in
psycho-analysis as well as in McDougall,
and English psychologists have followed
suit. Dr. Frank Watts, for instance,
interprets industrial unrest in terms
of Jung's theory of regression and the
complex, and of Freud's concepts
of mental conflict, repression, and the
unconscious.[2] Independent writers like

[1]Op. cit. Chap. I.

[2]Dr. Frank Watts, *An Introduction to the
Psychological Problems of Industry*, Chap. VI.

## ECONOMICS AND BEHAVIOUR

Thorstein Veblen, J. A. Hobson, and R. H. Tawney[1] have perceived the omission in economic textbooks of these psychological factors presumably so vital to economic welfare. When their weight is added, the attack upon economic theory cannot be summarily criticized as sheer quackery, nor can it be lightly dismissed according to established academic usage, and just cut.

[1] e.g. R. H. Tawney, *Acquisitive Society* , Chap. IX, C.

## III

### THE ECONOMISTS' DEFENCE

It is impossible to ignore McDougall's conclusion that " mankind is only a little bit reasonable, and to a great extent very unintelligently moved in quite unreasonable ways ".

Does modern economics, then, fall to the ground with the apparent collapse of its major premise of the human calculator ?

Professed economists, many of them, are not yet aware of this onslaught upon their means of livelihood, but in a few it has unquestionably aroused the instinct of self-defence, though the precise reaction takes various forms. Some maintain that the foundations have given way only under certain scattered portions of the economic structure ; others that the foundations have given way only to the extent of bringing down the top stories of the structure ; while yet others declare their independence, and maintain that the foundations that have given way were not under their structure at all.

Economists have supposed the central structure of economics to be limited to the " study of mankind in the ordinary business of life "[1], and that under this central pile the foundations hold. Though in the bosom of their family and under the influence of a festive season cost may be of ' no consideration ', and, giving rein to their parental or herd instinct, they may shower out presents obviously of no ' utility '

[1] This definition of economics forms part of the first sentence of Marshall's *Principles*. It is a most convenient and politic definition, since its reference can be changed by merely adjusting the intonation. If the word *business* is emphasized (though that word requires further definition) it satisfies those looking for something specific to study ; if the word *ordinary* is emphasized critics of economic narrowness are pacified. This latter intonation would make economics include the study of family life, social intercourse, etc. and would identify it with sociology ; but it is the implication of the alternate intonation that is being dealt with here.

to any one, business men are supposed in their business transactions to be inveterate calculators.

The housewife who buys provisions with a bare two or three pounds for a whole week's consumption by a large family, can hardly be supposed to be readily stimulated by objects other than the useful and cheap. If not by nature, she must be a calculator by bitter experience. Now the poor but thrifty housewife and the alert business man between them account for the bulk of purchases made on all commercial markets ; they have become the hero and heroine of an Economics willing to confine its attentions to the provision of a limited range of wants.

By such a cut in the plan of its structure economics stands exposed as the dismal science. To suppose that humankind seldom acts without a ' canny ' calculation of the amount of satisfaction to be derived and cost involved is dismal enough to some humanitarians or idealists and to all snobs ; but if it is only to be the cal-

culation about 'main-chances', pelf,
or £ s. d. by profit-making undertakers
and poverty-haunted housewives that
interests economics, clearly no cheer-
fully disposed fellow will touch it.[1]

And when economists in alternative
definitions describe their science as
the study of material wealth or material
welfare they confirm public opinion.
Housewife and business man are taken
to purchase only material goods and
services, and economics appears to
wallow in the material and 'lower'
things of life, blind (by arrangement)
to all that is spiritual and 'higher'. To
make matters worse mediaeval theology
has taught us to identify the material
with the bad, the spiritual with the

[1] Economics originally incurred the epithet
dismal because it was largely concerned
with the almost insoluble troubles of the
'deserving' poor, and because the laws it
set forth were of the nature of gloomy fore-
bodings. Even to-day economics maintains
that utility is always diminishing and likewise the returns from land. But if poverty
and these laws are true and not merely
assumptions it is the social, psychological,
and technical facts involved that are dismal.
not the economic science that must take
account of them.

54

good, a view that lingers in our speech and much of our thinking ; so that economics appears not merely dismal but vile.

Judgment based on outworn theological dichotomy need not, of course, deter the scientific economist, but his self-denying ordinance seems to me to restrict the scope of economics quite unnecessarily and quite fails to meet the attack of the instinct school. There are many material things—beer, assorted chocolates, plus fours, patent medicines—certainly no more, perhaps even less, subject to calculated buying than spiritual things like Bibles, pews, funerals, old masters, or Cook's tours.

If I exchange one lesson in French or etiquette with a socially ambitious barber's assistant for a dozen shaves, the terms of the exchange and what lies behind them are of great economic interest ; and if shaving and decency generally are considered as only next to godliness, certainly my lessons are not wholly materialistic. And suppose so many lessons in the higher theology are exchanged for so much time spent in performing the duties of a curate to a theological vicar ; are not the actual terms of the exchange of interest to the economist ? And surely these lessons and duties are not ' material ' !

Probably the economist has been over-modest in his protestations. Actually he does not confine himself only to the business side of life or to the prices only of material things, and an all-in policy seems justified by the similarity of the conditions observed and results obtained. There is no reason why the demand for, and the cost of, education, spiritual healing, knighthoods, or dramatic and orchestral performances should not also in the long run react upon the prices and terms of exchange of these commodities, at any rate among the well-to-do, capable of forming a cash-demand for amenities and luxuries.

As I write an announcement arrives of a book published under the title, *The Economic Laws of Art Production.*

## THE ECONOMISTS' DEFENCE

The author, Sir Hubert Llewellyn Smith, discusses such topics as the demand and the supply factor in the evolution and modification of artistic styles; short-period deviations (of fashion) from the style curve, and long-period trends; the effect on works of art of division of labour, machine industry, international intercourse; the effective demand for Art and the social conditions for a living Art Culture. Are these topics to be excluded from the economic purview? Works of art have an exchange-value, and if this diverges as widely from their aesthetic value as the exchange-value of water diverges from its physiological value there is all the more reason for studying *why*. Economics need only stop short at the price*less* or *in*valuable, and there seems no valid reason for neglecting the facts of exchange when its terms are non-material.

Instead of cutting up the structure vertically, leaving the more spiritual or sundry wings to others and retaining only the central ordinary business pile as his own domain, the economist may cut the premises up horizontally into flats and retain only the lower stories for himself. The economist may take up the position that economic laws and prognostications merely describe tendencies situated below, *underlying*, the actual course of events. To alter the metaphor, economic laws may be considered as general rules laid down by the legislature but subject to constant abrogation by administrative orders. Though on any average occasion officials are found to be acting on these administrative orders, their normal action may be said to be conditioned by general legislation.

"A normal price", writes Dr. Marshall, "is the price which any one set of conditions tends to produce. . . . It is only by accident that an average price will be a normal price".

There is no more vivid presentation of this conception than Marshall's own discussion of the significance of trade combinations, alliances, and counter-alliances among employers and employed, as well as among traders and manufacturers.[1]

> " They present a succession of picturesque incidents and romantic transformations, which arrest public attention and seem to indicate a coming change of our social arrangements now in one direction and now in another; and their importance is certainly great and grows rapidly. But it is apt to be exaggerated; for indeed many of them are little more than eddies, such as have always fluttered over the surface of progress. And though they are on a larger and more imposing scale in this modern age than before; yet now, as ever, the main body of movement depends on the deep silent strong stream of the tendencies of normal distribution and exchange; which ' are not seen ', but which control the course of those episodes which ' are seen '. For even in conciliation and arbitration, the central difficulty is to discover what is that normal level from which the decisions of the court must not depart far under penalty of destroying their own authority."

The difference between a normal tendency and an actual average will be readily intelligible to those who have experienced continental travel. Under

---

[1] Marshall, *Principles of Economics*, VI, viii, 10.

specified conditions of light, tide, and wind, the cross-channel steamer will be said to complete its journey in so many minutes. This is the normal time consumed. But if the actual time spent in crossing on a number of occasions were averaged it would probably be found to diverge considerably from the normal time—and that unfavourably to the susceptible. Conditions of light, tide, and wind seldom remain as favourable as specified, their vagaries are almost all in the obstructive direction and do not cancel out.

The contrast must be emphasized between what prices, wages, rents, profits, rates of interest would normally be if certain assumptions were satisfied and the *actual* moneys passing hands under these titles. The economist regards wages, profits, or interest, for instance, as the remuneration for labour, organizing ability, and waiting ; but it is seldom the case that any service paid for is purely that of waiting, without bearing some measure of risk, or purely that of organizing ability without being compounded of some labour and some waiting, as in the small shop-keeper's case. Nor does economic rent, the surplus of total revenue over cost of production, often correspond to any actual sum passing into the landlord's hands.

The English land-owning system, developed in the early nineteenth century proved a stimulating subject for economic thought for the very reason that the landlord, farmer, and labourer of the flesh almost corresponded to the Landowner, Entrepreneur, and Labourer of normal theory ; but in general the economist of the fundamentalist school confines his attention to the elemental forces *below* the surface only. He assumes certain conditions which probably will not account for everything in the superstructure of events, but which are sufficiently true to life to shape events in the long run. The conception of the calculating economic man with his principle of substitution, and the assumption of one price for similar articles in the same market are only two of these conditions. They would perhaps not affect events, even in the long run, if there were not other enabling conditions also assumed :

1. Reasonable knowledge of market conditions by those engaged in buying and selling.

2. Fair mobility of labour and capital in adjusting itself to demand ; though if immobility is held to exist new laws can be worked out, e.g. the theory of international trade.

3. Real competition among buyers and among sellers ; though, if monopoly is held to exist on one side only, new sets of economic laws can be framed to suit.

4. Divisibility of the commodity into enough units consumed and pro- duced, to make quantitative calculation and ' balancing ' possible.

5. A more or less stationary state, where (though everything may be increasing in volume) " by far the most important conditions of production and consumption, of exchange and dis-

tribution will remain of the same quality, and in the same general relations to one another"[1].

Obviously, however calculating man may be by nature, his ignorance, or the non-divisibility of commodities, or 'dynamic' changes (absence of assumptions 1, 4, or 5) will make calculation on his part futile. When all the assumptions are taken together they form a state of affairs distant enough from the actual conditions of the world to enjoin the subjunctive or conditional mood upon the economist. Instead of saying " exchange value in the long run tends to equal cost of production", it is accurate to say " if assumptions 1, 2, 3, 4, and 5 hold, then exchange value *would* tend, in the long run, to equal cost of production ".

The 'if' clause—the protasis of the grammarians—is usually represented in the actual statement of economic

[1] Marshall, *Principles of Economics*, V, v, 3.

laws by the phrase ' other things being equal ', and such statements often appear padded and circumscribed enough to excite derision. It is certainly questionable how far such statements, if true, are of any use in describing the facts of the world. The doctrines of deductive economics, like those of Euclidean geometry, are only *relative* to given conditions, and there may not be any facts occurring at all under the particular conditions prescribed.

The actual world—even merely the actual business world—is probably too varied and multiform to be adequately described by the permutations and combinations of the few variables allowed under the assumptions of invariable mobility, knowledge, competition, divisibility of units, and the stationary state. English deductive economics will probably soon have said all that there is to be said, and like the Austrian school will cease from new endeavour ; though to be sure a useful outlet for its thought may always be

## THE ECONOMISTS' DEFENCE

found in the writing of manuals, handbooks, textbooks, and other up-to-date popularizations of a fixed, authoritative gospel.

E

## A DECLARATION OF
## INDEPENDENCE

In contrast to those economists who execute a strategic retreat into the central core of the structure, or into its lower story, or both (i.e. confine themselves to general tendencies subjoined to given assumptions in the business and housekeeping world), are those Post-Marshallians who boldly assert that it is not the foundations of *their* scientific structure that have collapsed.

Economics and Psychology, writes Henderson,[1] are primarily concerned with different things.

> " People sometimes speak as though they supposed the economist to start from a few psychological assumptions (e.g. that a man is actuated mainly by his own self-interest) and to build up his theories upon such foundations by a process of pure reasoning. When, therefore, some advance in the study of psychology throws into apparent

Henderson, *Supply and Demand*, p. 1.

disrepute such ancient maxims about human nature, these people are disposed to conclude that the old economic theory is exploded, since its psychological premises have been shown to be untrue. Such an attitude involves a complete misunderstanding not merely of economics, but of the processes of human thought. It is quite true that the various branches of knowledge are interrelated very intimately, and that an advance in one will often suggest a development in another. By all means let the economist and psychologist avoid a pedantic specialism and let each stray into the other's province whenever he thinks fit. But the fact remains that they are primarily concerned with different things : and that each is most to be trusted when he is upon his own ground. When, therefore, the economist indulges in a generalization about psychology, even when he gives it as a reason for an economic proposition, in nine cases out of ten the economics will not depend upon the psychology ; the psychology will rather be an inference (and very possibly a crude and hasty one) from the economic facts of which he is tolerably sure."

This sounds good commonsense, but unfortunately for his case Henderson does not practise what he preaches, in fact cannot practise what he preaches. Throughout his book the reasoning is deductive, and he deduces his conclusions from psychological assumptions;

he cannot therefore argue without assuming some sort of psychological theory. I do not quarrel with the particular theory adopted, but the fact remains that it is psychological.

There is an example of Henderson's argument in practice, forty pages from his preaching, in which we are given a description of how a housewife when buying butter ' considers ', ' thinks ', ' hesitates ', ' weighs alternatives ', ' takes decisions ', ' sizes up ', and ' judges '—in almost consecutive sentences.[1] If this does not assume a psychological process of calculation and balancing one may as well abandon words for all but emotional purposes.

The fact is that economists, if they are to use deductive methods, cannot ignore psychology ; and in so far as the social psychology of McDougall is correct their house *has* collapsed, and Henderson is simply propping it up with a rival psychological theory.

[1] Henderson, *Supply and Demand*, pp. 41 and 42.

## A DECLARATION

Personally I admire Henderson's props—particularly for what they are *not* made of. It is noticeable that his verbs only imply calculation, they do not specify the terms in which calculations take place.

When a human being demands some article such as butter it is not necessarily implied that he, or let us say she, has consciously evaluated the exact sort of utility she expects to get out of its use. She may calculate, may balance the utility she expects against the price of the article without basing that expected utility on any rational consideration of the consequences. She simply *wants* the articles up to a certain price, and that want may be due to a clever advertisement (of a Maypole?), to a passing craze ('eat butter for your health'?), or to inborn instinct itself.

Economic theory assumes a balancing of utilities against costs, but it does not have to make any assumptions as to the *type of weights*, the states of mind, appetites, aversions, crotchets, *et. al.* thrown into the scale.

True, ' utility ' may suggest at first sight some sort of desirability or moral benefit and even, on second thought, desiredness or some conscious expectation of pleasure. The first impression cannot be too strongly repudiated by economists selecting and using their terms with a sense of scientific dignity ; the second impression takes too narrow a view of the sources of economic demand. Though psychologists have put forward words of greater refinement,[1] ' want ' is perhaps the most familiar word conveying approximately the right non-committal impression.

Utility should be used to refer simply

[1] I. A. Richards in his *Principles of Literary Criticism* objects to the word as suggesting too much of conscious desire, and proposes to substitute ' appetency '. R. H. Thouless objects to ' want ' as suggesting " the permanent tendency underlying an individual's demand for a particular commodity " rather than " a transitory condition underlying his demand for it at any particular moment ", and he proposes the word ' craving ' to refer to the latter which he correlates by definition with the " strength of seeking behaviour ".

to what people want, the quality of being wanted, either instinctively *or* rationally ; but though this is what the orthodox economic definition implies, economists apparently cannot restrain themselves from thinking most of the time of what reasonable persons (like themselves) consciously desire. They build their deductions from introspection, and often a heavily censored introspection at that ! There are also historical traditions behind this conception of *Homo sapiens*.

> Erect, with front serene, he stands
> A man, the lord and king of nature all.
> His large and arched brow sublime,
> Of wisdom deep declares the seat !

These eighteenth-century ideas—the passage is from an Aria in Haydn's *Creation* without sufficient Biblical authority—profoundly influenced the political economy that was growing into a system in that century.

Man was considered the model of wisdom :—

(A) In choosing wise Ends.

(B) In choosing the wisest Means to secure whatever his particular End.

## ECONOMICS AND BEHAVIOUR

In the early nineteenth century wisdom, type A, was being abandoned. The End was a wise or unwise enjoyment of pleasure, and the first paragraph of Bentham's *Principles of Morals and Legislation* lays down that it is for pain and pleasure alone " to determine what we shall do. . . . They govern us in all we do, in all we say, in all we think." And now, in the twentieth century, the time has come to abandon the theory of wisdom, type B.

Yet, though we can no longer suppose man to calculate in terms of a wisely estimated pleasure or pain, we can still hold fast to calculation. It is perfectly feasible to admit calculation in terms merely of *expected* and often foolishly expected pleasure and pain, or even on terms *unspecified* at the outset.

The first of these possible modifications is often indicated by Bentham himself. In *A Table of the Springs of Action* Bentham insists that " nothing but the expectation of the eventual enjoyment of pleasure in some shape, or of exemption from pain in some shape, can operate in the character of a *motive* ".[1]

The second of these modifications enjoins the use of utility and cost to refer to all wants or aversions, whether they are consciously recognized and felt as 'desires', or are instinctive and unrecognized. In the teeth of Henderson's preaching of aloofness, but in conformity with his practice, the economist may continue to make use of the psychological assumption of calculation.

But perhaps I have been unable to follow the social psychologist to the bitter end. Does he perchance mean that the majority of mankind buy and sell without any reference to the price asked or offered, or to the possible ' bargains ' elsewhere ? Is it his contention that when women react ' instinctively ' to the brightly coloured, fluffy, lacy, furry objects displayed in shop windows or in tasty, snappy

[1] Cf. Wesley C. Mitchell, " Bentham's Felicific Calculus ", *Political Science Quarterly*, XXXII, 2.

advertisements, they react without any consideration of their own or their husband's purses, or to prices noted in other shops or other advertisements ; that the typical reaction that brings on the majority of purchases (if it is not one of mere grabbing) runs to the tune of ' price no consideration ', ' book it whatever it is ', ' never mind the exes '? And is it their contention that when men react to the popping of corks, to froth, and good fellowship with a ' what's yours ' and ' have another ', without thought of the cost, it is their typical form of ' pattern reaction ' in the making of a purchase and the exchanging of goods and commodities ?

If this is the contention of social psychologists of course economics must in their view break down. But their writings and those of their economic disciples are not clear on this all-important point. Economics may yet preserve the assumption that price is considered in the majority or at least a quorum of transactions, and that calculation still subsists between

74

## A DECLARATION

utility or wants, and costs or aversions ;
provided, however, that there is no
commitment to specific forms of utility
or cost. There will, to be sure, be a
certain loss of definiteness in the terms
of the calculation, but this lack of
precision in the basis of deduction must
be counterbalanced by resort to induction from experiments and observed
occurrences.

An adequate defence, therefore, to
the psychologists' onslaught takes the
form of retreat toward more non-
committal terms from which to deduce,
supported by a counter-attack on
inductive lines. To ensure proper co-
ordination between these tactics, the
terms used in deduction must refer to
observable conditions or facts, eligible
as a basis for induction ; and here the
trend toward a behaviorist terminology may succour.

Modern philosophers appear unable
to define even pleasure itself or its
opposite (most exactly referred to
as discomfort) except in terms of
objective observable movements.

## ECONOMICS AND BEHAVIOUR

" Discomfort ", states Bertrand Russell,[1] " is a property of a sensation or other mental occurrence, consisting in the fact that the occurrence in question stimulates voluntary or reflex movements tending to produce some more or less definite change involving the cessation of the occurrence. Pleasure is a property of a sensation or other mental occurrence consisting in the fact that the occurrence in question either does not stimulate any voluntary or reflex movement, or, if it does, stimulates only such as tend to prolong the occurrence in question."

The economist, then, need only watch how far there are or are not voluntary or reflex movements tending to produce change or prolongation of the *status quo ante*. " A thing has utility whenever it is wanted and it is wanted whenever a human being is so constructed as to respond positively (in a seeking way) whenever it (directly or mediately) stimulates him."[2]

[1] Bertrand Russell, *Analysis of Mind.*
[2] Z. C. Dickinson, *Economic Motives.*

## A DECLARATION

Utility is simply the quality of being wanted, and to be wanted is to be sought, to stimulate seeking. Similarly disutility, unwantedness is the quality of being shunned. And when we deal with demand-price and supply-price rather than with utility or cost, degrees of stimulation or non-stimulation are objectively distinguishable in a person's behaviour. The stimulus and reaction take the form of prices and measured *amounts* of money, goods, or services. The pressure of the prospective buyers' or consumers' seeking is measured in the price bid ; the resistance in the prospective sellers' or producers' shunning is measured in the prices required to overcome resistance, to call out various amounts of response, and to turn non-response into a positive response to any given extent.

## V

## RE-ORGANIZATION AND REFORM

The new strategy clearly requires modifications in drill and new words of command ; and I venture to formulate a few terminological rules that will avoid dangerous commitments and alliances, and yet will maintain, as Dr. Marshall counsels, continuity with the practice of the past.[1]

*Rule* 1. *By ' demand ' economists shall refer to various amounts of an article (goods, services, factors of production, etc.) for units of which persons are able and willing to offer specified*

[1] " We must keep constantly in mind the history of the terms which we use ... we should be bound to keep our use of terms as much as possible in harmony with the traditions of the past ; in order that we might be quick to perceive the indirect hints and the subtle and subdued warnings, which the experiences of our ancestors offer for our instruction." Marshall, *Principles of Economics*, II, i. 2.

*amounts of other articles (usually a demand-price in money) in exchange.*

Demand, in short, should not be identified with mere utility, but should correspond with vendibility, i.e. utility to the extent to which the article can be sold. This distinction is vital where unequal distribution of wealth allows the rich to demand things of low utility to them at a higher price than the poor can demand necessities ; but in the heat of argument this distinction is often dropped overboard to be picked up later (when the argument is concluded) in a paragraph on the diminishing utility of money.[1]

*Rule 2. ' Utility ' shall refer to the quality of being wanted, or more precisely to the degree to which an article is wanted—its wantedness.*

This utility may arise from the physiological need for a certain amount of food, rest, clothing, or shelter ; or from the requirements of technical production such as the manufacturer's

[1] Cf. Henderson, *Supply and Demand*, Chap. I.

occasional desire for new machines to replace those worn out or obsolete, and his continuous desire for raw materials and fuel.

The want may be for something pleasurable or may be simply an escape from pain and mortification. It may be a 'conventional' necessity, as tobacco, the preservation of honour, a decent funeral, making Christmas presents, or smart even though uncomfortable clothes for one's wife.[1] Thus aspidistras are largely wanted for window-dressing, the outward and visible sign of respectability; and even food variants, such as white bread rather than brown, cater to points of working-class honour and prestige rather than to physiological needs.

The want may arise from religious, moral, or ethical impulses such as the

[1] Cf. Veblen (*Theory of the Leisure Class*) on vicarious consumption and conspicuous waste. Convention demands that a wife must be so inconveniently dressed as to make it clear that her husband can afford to support her in idleness; this panders to his vanity, but vicariously, so as not to impede *his* earning power.

want to present Bibles or petticoats to the heathen ; or the want may be in the economist's private opinion frivolous and even wicked, such as rivalry in ostentation, the itch to show class and good form, and a leaning toward orgies ; or the want may be foolish and mistaken, such as many a reaction of the gullible to a clever advertisement.

It is popularly supposed that modern American advertising methods have completely upset the economics apple (and marginal orange) cart. McDougall thinks that economists have neglected to take account of the suggestibility of men which renders the arts of the advertiser and the pushing of goods generally, so profitable and effective. These suppositions are true only if the desire created leads to unthinking purchase ' at any price ' (Cf. p. 74), or if economics requires demand to arise only from wants for goods or services which *when consumed* actually do give satisfaction. Most economists do not make this requirement,[1] though others, to be sure, fail to speak with one voice or with clear voices on the matter.

Confusion arises by failure to distinguish the psychological situation at the moment of possible exchange from the psychological and physical situation *in the course of* production and consumption. This important distinction is hardly recognized at all on the demand side.[2] The consumer's monetary demand-price for an article is no doubt usually based on former

[1] The distinction between the satisfaction a person will get from a thing and the intensity of his desire for it is drawn very clearly by Prof. Pigou (*Economics of Welfare*, Part 1, Chap. II), and he adopts 'desiredness' as a substitute for utility to refer to intensity of desire. Desiredness however retains the assumption of consciousness that is so objectionable to the psychologist, and for that reason I prefer the word 'wantedness'.

[2] Though generally admitted on the supply or production side. In slack trade when plant is not used to full capacity the manufacturer is for the moment eager to find markets and puts his supply price comparatively low; but if he properly calculates charges on account of idle overhead, his costs *in the course of* production are, per unit produced, comparatively high.

experience of its power to satisfy his wants in the course of its consumption. But in the case of articles bought for the first time as the result of an attrac-tive advertisement this basis does not exist ; and utility-at-purchase, the degree of satisfaction that buying would give, may diverge from utility-in-con-sumption, the degree of satisfaction in the course of consumption.

To maintain continuity in term-inology, utility should be allowed to refer both to the quality of being wanted and to the quality, occasionally assigned to the word by Marshall,[1] of satisfying that want. But if this latitude is allowed, the satisfaction referred to by utility should be restricted to satisfaction at purchase, whether or not it corresponds exactly to satis-faction in consumption. Advertising creates a want that is satisfied on the purchase of the article advertised as any

---

[1] " The total utility of a thing to anyone (that is, the total pleasure or other benefit it yields him)." Marshall, *Principles of Economics*, III, iii, 1. But Marshall also refers in the same section to utility and want as " correlative terms ".

other want is satisfied. The article may not satisfy in consumption any more than ' genuinely ' sold articles may if circumstances alter after purchase (e.g. a relative dies after purchase of gaily coloured frocks) ; and of course the article may not satisfy any of the deeper feelings, i.e. give what moralizing economists call ' *true* ' or ' *real* ' satisfaction : but these distinctions are beside the point and cannot help in elucidating the conditions of demand.

In short, the economist's ' utility ', forming the basis of the purchaser's demand, shall refer to wants or satisfactions of wants *at purchase* ; and these wants arise from psychological states of all sorts, without reference to their origin in advertisement or otherwise, to their reasonableness or ' conscious recognizability ', or to their results in consumption. Utility is not the opposite of futility, but is the quality of being (however unreasonably, unrecognizably, or unsuccessfully) *wanted* and sought ; and the Law of Diminishing Utility which Marshall rightly introduces as "this familiar and fundamental tendency of human nature" can be thus formulated : the utility of an additional unit of a thing to anyone, that is the degree to which it is wanted or sought, diminishes with every addition to his total stock of units.

*Rule* 3. *By ' supply ' economists may refer : (a) to the existing stock of things or of persons ready to do things, available either instantaneously or shortly, in various amounts for specified prices ; and (b) to the possibility of creating further amounts by means of production.*

And that involves overcoming costs.

*Rule* 4. *The ' costs of production ' shall stand for various physiological and psychological aversions against producing, or balances of aversions over wants towards producing.*

These costs are supposed to arise in the breasts of all producers whether they be labourers, ' experts ', managers, or the owners of the capital invested. " The discommodity of labour ", writes Dr. Marshall,[1] " may arise from bodily or mental fatigue, or from its being carried on in unhealthy surroundings, or with unwelcome associates, or from its occupying time that is wanted for recreation, or for social or intellectual pursuits. But whatever be the form of the discommodity, its intensity nearly always increases with the severity and duration of labour."

The cost of production in the work of the business manager and the expert —the engineer, lawyer, doctor, artist, academic—is largely the cost of learning by education and by experience to act not instinctively but intelligently ; a difficult process of kicking against the pricks. In business, there is also the uncertainty as to how the risks that are taken will fall out. This uncertainty appears almost as much an aversion to average human susceptibilities as learning ; and insurance or uncertainty-bearing is supposed to be paid for as a further element in production costs.

[1] Marshall, *Principles of Economics*, **IV**, i, 2.

## RE-ORGANIZATION AND REFORM

The cost of providing capital used to be named 'abstinence', but as this word proves difficult as an explanation of incomes often so conspicuously squandered[1] the word 'waiting' has been substituted. "Human nature being what it is, we are justified in speaking of the interest on capital as the reward of the sacrifice involved in the waiting for the enjoyment of material resources, because few people would save much without reward; just as we speak of wages as the reward of labour, because few people would work hard without reward."[2]

*Rule* 5. *The balancing of utilities against costs shall be studied as far as possible objectively in terms of stimulus and reaction under a given situation.*

---

[1] "My £1,200 then are given me as 'the reward of abstinence.' It strikes me upon this, that if I had not my £15,000 of Bank Stock I should be a good deal more abstinent than I am, and that nobody would then talk of rewarding me for it." John Ruskin on Prof. Fawcett's *Manual of Political Economy*.

[2] Marshall, *Principles of Economics*, IV, vii, 8.

## ECONOMICS AND BEHAVIOUR

Questions addressed to buyers and sellers as to their *feelings* or *calculations* need not be excluded any more than the medical practitioner avoids questioning his patients as to their aches and pains, yet recitals of symptoms and verbal reactions generally shall always be suspect.

The cost of efforts of a given kind may be tested objectively by offering various payments for various hours of given work and observing how the labourer responds. It is academically correct to maintain that ' labour ' will exert itself for an hour or two for next to no payment, for the sake of the exercise. ' Labour's' reaction to such a proposition is more likely to be merely a vocal response, i.e. language ; but the payment of additional over-time rates that is now the usual practice in industry is perhaps a confirmation of the academic's further conception of a fatigue increasing disproportionately to the duration of labour.

The supposed cost of the capitalist's sacrifice in waiting, i.e. the supply-price of capital, also requires testing objectively. It may simply be a fiction, convenient, and comforting to the rich man's soul, but refutable by observation of the change in savings, if any, as rates of interest are experimentally reduced or increased.

The market or shopping ' situation ', again, presents man or woman with a ' stimulus ' to which he or she can respond by paying money (measured to the last farthing perhaps) ; and if the prices asked are increased it shall be observed at which point in the continuous series of prices the act of buying a given quantity by one or several individuals changes into not buying all that quantity. It is the exact price at which exchanging changes into not-exchanging a given quantity, that shall be referred to as the *marginal demand-price* for that quantity. Conversely if the *quantities offered at a given price* per unit are increased it shall be observed at what quantity in the continuous series the change will occur between payment and non-

payment for all units. The additional
unit that changes exchanging into not-
exchanging all units at the given price
per unit shall be referred to as the
*marginal unit demanded* at that price.

Henderson's contention that economics and psychology are concerned
with different things is clearly dis-
allowed by these rules. Economics is
concerned with the actions and behaviour of human beings, and so is
psychology ; and though economics
concentrates primarily on the terms of
only one form of human action, the
transaction of exchange, these terms
are largely determined by complicated
psychological factors. Economic costs
are as deeply rooted in the frailty and
fancies, the pricks, susceptibilities, and
impatience of human nature, they are
as physiological and psychological in
their origin, as economic utilities.
And the supply as well as the demand
side of his analysis leads the economist
to interpret the surface facts of exchange
in terms of the psycho-physiological

states of human producers and consumers.

This process of delving through a series of levels down to that of human nature is particularly evident in the discussion of the law of increasing costs—in this context equivalent to decreasing returns—operative in certain industries (notably agriculture) most of the time, and in most industries some of the time, i.e. in the short period. This law as applied to land is stated on any one of the three levels, the physical, the financial, or the psycho-physiological.

I. An increase in hours of labour, tons of manure, cubic yards of glasshouses, bushels of seeds, etc. applied to a given piece of land will add a less than proportionate return in the physical output, i.e. in bushels of wheat, pounds of pork, gallons of milk.

II. An increase in the financial expenses on account of capital and labour applied to a given piece of land will add a less than proportionate return in the money value of the produce.

## ECONOMICS AND BEHAVIOUR

III. An increase in the psycho-physiological effort or sacrifice (i.e. in the *real* costs of labour and capital) applied to a given piece of land will add a less than proportionate return in utility and the satisfaction of wants.

The law is usually stated as belonging exclusively to level I. " The return to capital and labour now under discussion is measured by the *amount* of the produce raised independently of any changes that may meanwhile take place in the exchange value or price of produce."[1]

But " when the tendency to Diminishing Return is generalized, the return is apt to be expressed in terms of value and not of quantity. . .The older method of measuring return in terms of quantity often jostled against the difficulty of rightly interpreting a dose of labour and capital without the aid of a money measure."[2]    Level II of

[1] Marshall, *Principles of Economics*, **IV**, ii, 4.
[2] Marshall, *Principles of Economics*, **IV**, iii, 8.

prices and finance must usually be the economist's *point d'appui*, but if he is to be something more than a mere business man he must attempt to reach level III.

"When considering costs from the social point of view, when inquiring whether the cost of attaining a given result is increasing or diminishing with changing economic conditions, then we are concerned with the real costs of efforts of various qualities, and with the real cost of waiting. If the purchasing power of money, in terms of effort has remained about constant, and if the rate of remuneration for waiting has remained about constant, then the money measure of costs corresponds to the real costs : but such a correspondence is never to be assumed lightly."[1]

These statements of tendencies toward diminishing return are simply the exact quantitative presentation of man's fight against nature ; against his own

[1] Marshall, *Principles of Economics* V, iii, 7.

reproductive, frail, prickly, susceptible, and impatient nature so liable to children, fatigue, obstinacy, panics, unrest, and improvidence ; as well as against the niggardliness or mal-distribution of resources in the external material world.

And economics does not stop short at counting the odds against man, but describes his more or less success-ful methods of organizing and fighting. Increasing population after a point renders the fight more difficult, but man's recent application of science to industry and the power of increasing the return from a given cost by large scale production has to some extent prevailed in adapting nature more tolerably to the growing desires of a growing number. And mutual re-criminations among the parties engaged in this adaptation are supposedly, though only gradually, instilling the need for forbearance, for a ' new spirit ' in industry, and generally for more peaceable industrial relations.

It is an heroic, stirring theme fit

for an epic, and yet an everyday, human-interest story fit for common proverbs and children's tales. Indeed the recent attempts to illustrate economics by texts from such a household favourite as *Alice in Wonderland* is no mere *tour de force* but a most appropriate reminder of man's inconsequence.

Economic terminology must allow the widest latitude to the vagaries of human striving and human aversions. The custom of Madingley where

" Things are done you'd not believe "

is more usual than that of Grantchester :

" The women there do all they ought
The men obey the Rules of Thought."

And Rupert Brooke is right to deem his own village unique.

The unaided reason of economists cannot possibly cope with the infinite possibilities of man's behaviour ; economists must continually take precautions against rational assumptions by recourse to the teachings of fairy-tales, nursery rhymes, and nonsense jingles. And the more elementary such stories, the more precaution the economist may imbibe. Take *Reading Without Tears*, from which I first learnt my spelling, and see what lessons in the cool contemplation of human disasters and folly the economist may draw when seeking for words to explain the adjustment of industrial relations to the needs of a growing population.

TEXT FOR THE INTRODUCTORY CHAPTER.
*Population and the Tendency to Over-reproduce.*

" Six lads will vis-it us
Go to the lar-der
Get a leg of mut-ton
Get six tur-nips."[1]

TEXT FOR THE SECOND CHAPTER.
*Industrial Depressions.*

" Jack will clam-ber up high trees.
Jack got to the top of the fir-tree
But he was diz-zy, and he fell and
snap-ped his neck."[2]

TEXT FOR THE THIRD CHAPTER.
*Labour Problems and Industrial Unrest.*

" My dog is in his ken-nel.
Un-tie him. He will fol-low me.
He has bit-ten a rab-bit.
Tie him up. Pat him on his back."[3]

---

[1] *Reading Without Tears*, Part I, p. 179.
[2] Op. cit. p. 213.
[3] Op. cit. p. 167.

# RE-ORGANIZATION AND REFORM

TEXT FOR THE FOURTH CHAPTER.
*Strikes and Strike-breakers.*

" James drop-ped his hat in the riv-er.
Tray seiz-ed it and laid it at the feet of
James.
James pat-ted Tray on the back.
Tray nev-er bites, but he licks.
Tray has black legs."[1]

TEXT FOR THE FIFTH CHAPTER.
*The Plan of Profit Sharing.*

" Tom has got a bit of mut-ton.
Tom will give a wee bit to Joe."[2]

TEXT FOR THE SIXTH CHAPTER.
*Welfare Work.*

" Get a big can of tea.
Make a big cake. Bake it well.
Cut it up in ten bits.
Let Jack bl-ow a trum-pet."[3]

TEXT FOR THE SEVENTH AND
LAST CHAPTER.
*Conciliation and Arbitration ; Appointment
of Royal Commissions.*

" Sit still on the sti-le, till I get a tile for
you to st-ep up-on."[4]

[1] Op. cit. p. 243.
[2] Op. cit. p. 165.
[3] Op. cit. p. 220. Jack was the Entre-preneur himself ; see text for Chapter the Second.
[4] Op. cit. p. 255.

## VI

## COUNTER-ATTACK

Renouncing all a priori general
assumptions of their own about human
springs to action, economists may now
turn upon the social psychologists.
What agreement have they reached
upon the nature of human nature
that might serve as a basis for deductive
prognostications ?

The number and description of
innate instincts identified will, at
the very outset, be found to vary
with different authorities. Indeed, what
one school calls an innate instinct
another calls a consolidation of instinct
and habit. Watson, in the course
of careful observation, was not able to
detect more than three instincts in
new-born babies—fear, rage, and love.
He points out that animals which
have the most complete instinctive
equipment, the insects, for example

have the least capacity for habituation and learning ; and those with largest learning capacity seem to have fewest instincts. This inverse relationship between learning power and instinct suggests important reservations in applying theories of instinct to the behaviour of man, the supreme learner.

In fact the new 'social' psychology of McDougall is heavily beset by a psychology yet newer, the Behaviorism of Watson, which pays increasing attention to habits and habit-formation. The instincts distinguished and harped upon by the social psychologists are dismissed by this school as a mere classification of the multifarious varieties of human behaviour into a few more easily grasped types of behaviour ; a 'standardization' that is convenient and possibly necessary, but not an interpretation. Interpretation must come, according to the Behaviorist school, by reference to habit-formation and the conditioned reflex. A dog may be made to lick his chops and to 'salivate' at the

mere sound of a dinner gong un-
accompanied by a meal, if the gong
on a sufficient number of previous
occasions has actually been accompanied by food. Salivation is no longer
an instinctive form of behaviour, but a
reflex habit conditioned by the specific
custom or institution of the gong
before food ; a habit whose formation
can be observed in the case of each
individual, step by step, historically
and inductively.

May not economics draw a moral
from this Behaviorist trend ? The
facts that come within the purview of
economics are those of exchange, an
activity of men and bodies of men
which is intricately bound up with
social or political customs and institutions that have grown up ' historically ', and often independently of the
economic activity they may now appear
to subserve. Could not a Behaviorist
institutional science be developed to
describe and interpret human organization, less snobbish and priggish
than the political science of the ancient,

mediaeval, and modern schools? As Mr. G. D. H. Cole and Prof. H. J. Laski have urged so forcefully, all human societies must be admitted to the precincts hitherto reserved to Church and State. And the actual institutions and behaviour, the actual customs and doings of people should be noticed, not other people's ideas of what they ought to do, nor yet clauses of paper constitutions stating merely what thay are supposed to do.

Mr. and Mrs. Sidney Webb have shown the way in their meticulous examination of trade unions, local authorities, co-operative societies, and charitable bodies ; and the same systematic analysis can be extended to business and industrial organizations —manufacturing firms, commercial houses, banks, monopolistic trusts, and the looser co-operation of middlemen, brokers, and agents on the market.

Social and historical circumstances must no longer be regarded merely as an ornamental frame to the picture of price-changes and terms of exchange, but as a background within the picture ; as factors augmenting or limiting supply, stimulating or checking demand, and thus highly relevant to the main economic issue. Indeed, orthodox economics seems to have been most accurate and most successful in its forecasts where, as in banking and taxation problems, it has stooped to study the actual social organizations involved.

Economics has probably more to learn from such sciences of social behaviour as anthropology, constitutional history, comparative politics, and administrative theory than it has from any social psychology of instincts, even if this psychology were a compact and consistent body of knowledge—which it is not.

Whether the innate instincts of man be few or many, whether or not they are instincts so much as compositions of instinct and habit, no method has to my knowledge been suggested of fusing these several forces

in the same way that the conception
of the ' margin ' and ' equilibrium '
compounds the forces of supply and
demand.   Even if it were true, therefore, that purchases and sales on the
market are made by instinct we could
deduce nothing.   Writers like Carleton
Parker and Ordway Tead, though
they have interpreted various actions
in terms of single instincts, have
never seriously attempted a synthesis.

Supposing one instinct is opposed
by another, is there any information
to indicate which is the stronger ?

If economics were really to be a
deduction from fifteen or seven or
even three independent and often
warring instincts, its last state would
be something like Bacon's physiological
system as interpreted by Mr. Shandy,
senior, in terms of spirit, air, heats,
and humours.[1]

> " The two great causes which con-
> spire with each other to shorten life, says
> Lord Verulam, are first :—
> " The eternal spirit, which, like a
> gentle flame, wastes the body down to

[1] Sterne, *Tristram Shandy*, Book V,
Chap. xxxv.

103

death : And secondly, the external air, that parches the body up to ashes : which two enemies attacking us on both sides of our bodies together, at length destroy our organs, and render them unfit to carry on the functions of life.

" This being the state of the case, the road to Longevity was plain ; nothing more being required, says his Lordship, but to repair the waste committed by the internal spirit, by making the substance of it more thick and dense, by a regular course of opiates on one side, and by refrigerating the heat of it on the other, by three grains and a half of salt-petre every morning before you got up.

" Still this frame of ours was left exposed to the inimical assaults of the air without ; but this was fenced off again by a course of greasy unctions, which so fully saturated the pores of the skin, that no spicula could enter ;—nor could any get out. This put a stop to all perspiration, sensible and insensible, which being the cause of so many scurvy distempers, a course of clysters was requisite to carry off redundant humours, and render the system complete."

Is not this quite in the vein of Carleton Parker's creatures of instinct ?[1] But the sort of thing Francis Bacon actually wrote[2] was very different from either Shandy or Parker.

[1] Above page 42.
[2] Francis Bacon, *Of the Advancement of Learning*, Second Book.

## COUNTER-ATTACK

" And for the humours, they are
commonly passed over in anatomies as
purgaments ; whereas it is most necessary
to observe what cavities, nests, and
receptacles the humours do find in the
parts, with the differing kind of humour
so lodged and received. And as for the
footsteps of diseases, and their devasta-
tions of the inward parts, imposthuma-
tions, exulcerations, discontinuations,
putrefactions, consumptions, contractions, extensions, convulsions, disloca-
tions, obstructions, repletions, together
with all preternatural substances, as
stones, carnosities, excrescences, worms,
and the like ; they ought to have been
exactly observed by the multitude of anatomies and the contribution of men's
several experiences, and carefully set
down both historically according to the
appearances, and artificially with a
reference to the diseases and symptoms
which resulted from them, in case
where the anatomy is of a defunct
patient ; whereas now upon opening of
bodies they are passed over slightly and
in silence."

And this gives us our clue.

Let us " exactly observe " a " multitude " of cases, contribute our several
experiences, and carefully " set down "
the " appearances and symptoms "
whether they be physiologic or economic
discontinuations, consumptions, and
contractions, and *then* proceed to the
explanation of the humours.

105

## ECONOMICS AND BEHAVIOUR

And this in fact has been the course
consistently pursued by at least one
of the classical economists—Malthus.
Malthus's essential doctrine did not
depend on any psychological assumption, and certainly not that of the
human calculator. The positive checks
—the high death rates—Malthus *observed* to have operated so powerfully
throughout the ages, in wars, pest-
ilences, and famines, were essentially
the result of man's inconsequence
and incontinence, his *lack* of calculation.
Indeed, it is said to have been Malthus's
theory that first suggested to Darwin
the principle of natural selection applicable to all life, animal and vege-
table.[1]

[1] " In October, 1838, that is fifteen months
after I had begun my systematic inquiry,
I happened to read for amusement Malthus on
Population, and being well prepared to
appreciate the struggle for existence which
everywhere goes on, from long-continued
observation in the habits of animals and
plants, it at once struck me that under
these circumstances favourable variations
would tend to be preserved, and unfavourable
ones to be destroyed." Darwin's *Auto-
biography*, quoted by W. T. Layton in an
Introduction to Malthus's *Essay on Population*,
Everyman's Library Edition.

## COUNTER-ATTACK

Since Malthus's time, and Malthus died in 1834, few economists have followed his method. Dr. Keynes in his *Scope and Method of Political Economy*, written in 1890, tells us that " political economy, whether having recourse to the deductive method or not, must both begin with observation and end with observation",[1] but this appears more in the nature of a pious wish than a description of the actual practice of economists.

Works on economics which start with accurately measured observations of fact are still the exception, but among them may be numbered the investigations of Professor A. L. Bowley, Sir Josiah Stamp, and Mr. Seebohm Rowntree, W. T. Layton's *Introduction to the Study of Prices*, Sir William Beveridge's *Unemployment*, Prof. H. L. Moore's monographs on wages, cycles, price-forecasting, and Prof. Wesley C. Mitchell's *Business Cycles*. The modern investigation of the business

[1] J. N. Keynes, *Scope and Method of Political Economy*, Chap. VII.

107

cycle is indeed the leading case of
the method I am advocating. Such
inquiries start out with accurate statistics of the prices of goods and services,
market values of stocks and shares,
rates of interest and profit, and reduce
the fluctuations observed in the figures
to index numbers and other statistical
summaries of events. Explanation
follows *after* the general trend of
the facts is ascertained and the situation
analysed ; it does not anticipate and
abrogate observation, as though the
facts were the invariable manifestation
of psychological certainties already
analysed.

Indeed, I might suggest ' Cycle-
Analysis not Psycho-Analysis ' as a
suitable slogan for this new economics, if
this were not perhaps unfair to psycho-
analysis as commonly understood. In
its everyday practice this psycho-
analysis starts and proceeds by the
most intensive and patient observation,
and is comparable to the old economics
only when speculating philosophically
beyond these observations upon Hamlet

and human behaviour generally, in fiction and fact.

Statistical methods of investigation into economic questions other than that of the cycle, appear to be making headway in America,[1] but not in England. A beginning was made with statistical answers to such questions as the extent to which the human factor affects industrial efficiency ;[2]

[1] See essays in the *Trend of Economics*, (New York, 1925) by W. C. Mitchell, F. C. Mills, and others. Official investigations by statistical methods contained, e.g. in the Bulletins of the U.S. Department of Labor or the Census of Manufactures, show a remarkable advance, and attention should be drawn to the work and publications of the Harvard Committee on Economic Research, the National Bureau of Economic Research, the Institute of Economics, and the Pollak Foundation for Economic Research. The organization of these Bureaus is described by Prof. Z. C. Dickinson in the *Economic Journal*, Sept., 1923.

[2] Cf. my *Economics of Fatigue and Unrest* (London, 1924). It is not generally realized what a variety of objective tests of efficiency are at hand—labour turnover, lost time, accidents, quantity and quality of output, etc.—nor yet what a variety of measurable conditions there are— hours of work, amounts and methods of pay, hygiene, etc.—that can be tested.

but the contempt for knowledge, the traditionalism, and the short-sightedness of the typical English business man, the economy campaigns of successive governments,[1] and the paucity of Universities willing or able to support social research have proved insuperable obstacles. In spite of repeated urgings by the master himself and by Dr. Keynes, his near contemporary, the successors of Dr. Marshall are as far from adopting statistical methods as were his predecessors. Economics in England appears to be receding further into its shell; spending less time than ever on the investigation of the outside world, and ever more time in most systematically sealing itself in.

[1] Statistical Blue-Books cost anything from three to five times their pre-war price. Other blue-books vital to the social statistician have been entirely discontinued. The ' axe ' has also been applied on many grants to boards and departments engaged in research and the collection of statistical material.

# VII

## CONCLUSIONS

Orthodox economics still involves, and often starts out with, a priori conceptions of human behaviour based on the balancing of wants against the costs of effort or sacrifice. This conception of the 'human calculator' is, according to modern social psychology, largely untrue; but it is a highly convenient conception from which to make deductions. The conception of man as a non-calculating creature of numerous instincts or of compositions of instinct and habit, is considerably less convenient and probably no more true to life. In a sufficient proportion of their activities, particularly the economic activity of buying and selling, a sufficient proportion of persons do usually appear to calculate, though not necessarily in terms of pleasure or pain, moral benefit or conscious desire. People certainly do not all and always react or respond to stimulus quite regardless of cost and price in the same way as, for instance, they make responses in Church ; and the exploitation by the psychological school of a ' normal ' instinctive animal for deductive purposes, stands condemned as no better scientifically than the orthodox use, for the same purpose, of a ' normal ' economic man. To discover what general, powerful instincts reside in man and what is their relative force, and then to deduce from this how men will act (if at all) under given circumstances (that may never arise) is equally topsy-turvy and equally fallacious.

The way out of the dilemma is to drop deduction from *any* a priori view of human nature as the main source of economic knowledge. Economics, and social research generally, must stand on their own feet. Instead of being treated like babes in arms fed out of bottled psychology, they

## CONCLUSIONS

must collect their own pabulum in the highways and by-ways of life. Modern psychology has developed and won respect as a result of collecting facts for itself. Let economics go and do likewise.

Induction by means of experiment under selected and controlled conditions such as are provided by a laboratory, is usually excluded by the circumstances of social organization and activities. These can hardly be tampered with for mere economics' sake, any more than can the motions of the stars for the sake of astronomy. As a substitute for the laboratory, recourse must be had to statistical methods. This does not mean more mathematics unintelligible to the average reader, but rather the displacing of pure mathematics of the differential calculus type, by mathematics which the professional mathematician considers so easy as hardly to deserve the name.

The possibilities of statistical measurement are scarcely realized by most economists, who seem content to reiterate old deductions, and are too busy or too bored to explore the way of exact observation, or to use the wealth of statistical material put at their disposal by government departments, Royal Commissions, German and American Universities, and some few research institutes. These statistics show clearly the Alice-in-Wonderland variability, changeability, uncertainty, and interrelations of human behaviour. And there are easy mathematical devices that sum up variations in behaviour (say strikes of wage-earners) by means of averages and frequency distributions, that sum up changes and tendencies, estimate risks and uncertainties, and find some measure of association or correlation between the values of two or more variable characters, say a person's strike-behaviour and the wage he earns.

These measuring devices are mere instruments. Like agricultural tools they cannot be successfully applied without judgment and skill and a

## CONCLUSIONS

knowledge of conditions ' in the field '. Statistical *mathematics* must be preceded, guided, and reviewed by statistical *fieldwork* : the selection and definition of the terms, samples, and indices by which to describe the points at issue ; orientation as to all the possible and probable factors influencing those issues and likely to influence them in unobserved cases generally ; and isolation of factors to test the particular and general force of any such hypothetical influence in the unknown past and future.

This is the cue for economic theory to play its part. Though verification and proof of any generalization or law applicable to unobserved cases (and often its original suggestion) comes by testing accurately observed factors, an hypothesis deduced from classical or current psychological doctrine may be a useful stage in the course of the investigation.

Observations and records of facts, however thorough their measurement by the latest statistical methods, will seldom, of and by themselves, give the true interpretation.[1] Two sets of facts found statistically to be correlated, such as marriages and the consumption of beer year by year, are not necessarily cause and effect, and to interpret their relation as such involves an hypothesis. Now theories, such as those of orthodox economics, if formulated in statistically measurable terms and steered clear of ethical implication, are perhaps the most plausible working hypotheses with which to start interpreting the measured facts. And the discussions about these theories, often carried on for generations, may suggest what units to measure by, what factors are relevant and irrelevant to the argument, and what issues require special investigation before any hypoth-

[1] The limitations of the statistician who works in isolation, ignorant of the economist's interpretation, are particularly patent in recent contributions to the theory of population. Cf. my *Over-population, Theory and Statistics*, Psyche Miniatures, Kegan Paul, 1926.

## CONCLUSIONS

esis can definitely be considered proved or disproved.

To qualify for this rôle theories about human reactions, institutions, and behaviour generally, must avoid the dogmatic psychological assumptions already criticized. Theoretical, hypothetical 'constructions' must be made, but these need not resemble Towers of Babel soaring into the air from the uncertain quicksands of psychological speculation. The necessary construction resembles rather a bridge starting from one solid bank of statistically summarized facts and ending on a further bank equally solid. The bridge is supported, perhaps, by speculative arguments as piers, but it cannot be entirely dependent thereupon—and hold.

### FINIS

For Product Safety Concerns and Information please contact our EU
representative GPSR@taylorandfrancis.com Taylor & Francis Verlag GmbH,
Kaufingerstraße 24, 80331 München, Germany


Printed and bound by CPI Group (UK) Ltd, Croydon, CR0 4YY
08/05/2025
01864382-0001